Chefs' Special

Rajasthani Kitchen

Chefs' Special

Rajasthani Kitchen

Pushpita Singh

Lustre Press
Roli Books

Acknowledgments

This book has been a lot of fun for me to write. For every recipe that was included, there were at least as many food-tasting parties with friends as victims!

I first learned to cook Rajasthani food after I was married, to please a fastidious family less than pleased with the more cosmopolitan culinary skills I grew up with in Calcutta.

My initiation into Rajasthani cooking was through my mother-in-law, Nawal Kanwar, who cooks little, but cooks it well. My primary thanks go to her. My sister-in-law, Usha Singh who is fast and efficient in the kitchen, innovates and adapts marvellously, and should have written this book. I thank her too for her valuable inputs. My sister, Amrita Singh, married into a Jaipur family known for its gourmet cooking, has helped me with some of the more difficult recipes.

My recipe research also took me to the chefs of Jaipur hotels, in particular The Welcomgroup Rajputana Sheraton and The Rambagh Palace, and to Mrs Mahavir Singh who shared some of her culinary insights with me, a stranger at her door! I greatly appreciate the fact that they shared their cooking secrets with me.

Flavours of Rajasthan

Rajasthan is rich in courtesies, its hospitality as well known as its codes of honour and chivalry. In a desert, where little is available, the choice of foodstuffs is always somewhat limited. This is what singles out the cuisine of India's desert state—the magic of creating a variety of tastes from very little.

The Rajput is a meat eater, but is by no means a committed non-vegetarian. Vegetarian food too forms a large part of the diet. When the rest of the country follows a strict vegetarian protocol during the celebration of Navratri, the festival of nine nights, the Rajput offers the goddess a goat as sacrifice. On all nine days, a similar offering is made, and the cooked meat eaten as blessed food.

Accompaniments like *kadhi*, more popularly known as *khatta*, form a part of the staple diet. Common vegetables are *sangri* and *gwarphali*, cooked in yoghurt. *Papads*, eaten roasted elsewhere in India, are eaten gravied in Rajasthan, as is *bhujiya*, a popular moth-lentil snack. Chickpea flour can be freshly rolled out as dumplings to make *gatte ka saag*, while sun-dried moth-lentil dumplings are also cooked as *badi ka saag*. These are eaten with either *bajre ki rotis*, or a porridge called *khichra*.

The Rajput sweet tooth is catered for on the *thaal*, the round plate on which the meal is served, in the form of *seera*, a *halwa* made of cooked wheat flour in clarified butter (*ghee*), or *lapsi*, a porridge made with desiccated grains of wheat, the latter usually reserved for auspicious occasions. Wedding feasts usually include sweetened yellow rice as a delicacy. Milk-based sweets like *barfi* are popular too.

Ker, a hard desert berry, is often added to pickles, or *sangri*, or cooked on its own. The amount of chillies used is somewhat more curtailed, and mango powder (*amchur*) and mustard seeds (*rai*) seem to have a dominating presence. Garlic is favoured in Rajput cooking. The consumption of milk, buttermilk and yoghurt forms a part of the main diet.

Daal-bati-choorma is a speciality of this region. The *daal* consists of a lentil curry; *bati* is a round ball of bread baked in a charcoal fire with clarified butter (*ghee*) concealed within; *choorma* is a sweet dish made with bread, bruised with jaggery or sugar and clarified butter (*ghee*).

A Rajasthani delicacy, linked with the monsoon festival of Teej, is called *ghevar*, consisting of round cakes of white flour over which sweetened syrup is poured. Muslim foods such as kebabs, *pasandas* and *sevaiyan* also occupy a place of pride in the overall cuisine of the state.

Most ingredients mentioned in the book are now easily available in shops not only in India, but also in major metros elsewhere, in their speciality Indian stores. If not, close equivalents may be substituted, as suggested in the recipes. Many of the recipes here are familiar to every Rajasthani household, but there are some that are less known like the game recipes, now dying out, since shikar is forbidden. The author has adapted some of these to lamb and chicken with successful results.

Rajasthani cuisine is not difficult to cook. Crisp, tangy, nutritious, spicy and wholesome — take 100 gm of adventurous spirit, deep fry in 10 tbsp of enthusiasm, season with a pinch of experimentation and create your own Rajasthani gourmet delight!

Commonly Used Rajasthani Ingredients

Papad: Flat, sun-dried wafers made from moth beans (*moth dal*) paste. These are eaten fried or roasted as snacks, and gravied as a main course dish.

Mangodi: Small sun-dried dumplings made from green gram (*moong*) or moth beans (*moth dal*) paste.

Kachri: A sour, cucumber-like vegetable from the melon family, it is sliced and stored dried. It acts as a tenderiser for lamb dishes and provides tanginess to the dishes.

Ker: A berry found on the desert trees. When fresh it is used to make pickles and in its dried form, is combined with *sangri* as an authentic vegetable preparation.

Sangri: This is a bean-like vegetable. Regarded as a delicacy, it is usually stored after it is dried.

Garam masala: Grind together the following spices: 75 gm cumin seeds (*jeera*), 5 bayleaves (*tej patta*), 5 black cardamoms (*bari elaichi*), 15 gm cloves (*laung*), 3 cinnamon sticks (*dalchini*), 15 gm black peppercorns (*sabut kali mirch*). Pass the mixture through a sieve and then store in an airtight jar.

Panch phoran: 5 gm fenugreek seeds (*methi dana*), 5 gm cumin seeds (*jeera*), 5 gm fennel seeds (*saunf*), 5 gm mustard seeds (*sarson*), 5 gm onion seeds (*kalonji*). Combine these spices and store.

Chat masala: Mix together the following: 5 gm mango powder (*amchur*), 5 gm black salt powder (*kala namak*), 5 gm roasted cumin seed (*bhuna jeera*) powder, 5 gm red chilli powder and 5 gm asafoetida (*hing*) powder.

Safed Maas
Exotic lamb curry

Preparation time: 30 min.
Cooking time: 1 hr.
Serves: 4-6

Ingredients:

Lamb, cut into pieces	1 kg
Salt to taste	
Yoghurt (*dahi*)	1¼ cups / 250 gm
Clarified butter (*ghee*)	1 cup / 200 gm
Green cardamoms (*choti elaichi*)	6-8
Cloves (*laung*)	5-6
Cinnamon (*dalchini*) sticks	3-4
Onions, big, sliced	3
Ginger (*adrak*), 3" pieces, shredded	2
White peppercorns (*sabut safed mirch*), powdered	15-20
Red chilli seeds, powdered	2 tbsp / 30 gm
Poppy seeds (*khuskhus*), ground	2 tbsp / 30 gm
Coconut (*nariyal*), powdered	2 tbsp / 30 gm
Wholemilk fudge (*khoya*), grated	½ cup / 100 gm
Almonds (*badam*), blanched, cut	15
Cashewnuts (*kaju*)	10
Garlic (*lasan*), ground to paste	3 pods
Saffron (*kesar*)	a pinch
Milk	1 tbsp / 15 ml
Whole red chillies (*sabut lal mirch*), deseeded	6-8

Method:

1. Boil the lamb in water with 2 tbsp of salt for 10 minutes.
2. Discard the water, and transfer the lamb pieces onto a flat dish. Smear the pieces with yoghurt.

3. Heat the clarified butter; add the green cardamoms, cloves, cinnamon and onions. Fry till the onions turn translucent. Add the ginger and fry for 1-2 minutes.
4. Add the lamb pieces, white peppercorns and red chilli seeds. Cook for 45 minutes on a low flame.
5. Add the poppy seeds and coconut powder and simmer for 15-20 minutes. Add the wholemilk fudge and stir the lamb.
6. Add the almonds and cashewnuts and then cook until the lamb is almost done.
7. Add the garlic paste. Cook on a slow fire till done.
8. Add the saffron soaked in 1 tbsp of milk, mix well. Garnish with the deseeded skins of red chillies and serve.

Meaty Tip!
Never refreeze meat that has been thawed out as it will turn hard and tough while cooking.

Hari Mirch Ka Maas
Spicy lamb curry

Preparation time: I hr. 30 min.
Cooking time: I hr.
Serves: 4-6

Ingredients:

Lamb, boneless pieces	1 kg
Yoghurt (*dahi*)	1 cup / 200 gm
Salt to taste	
Cumin seeds (*jeera*), powdered	2 tsp / 10 gm
Oil	1½ cups / 300 ml
Onions, sliced	1¼ cups / 250 gm
Water	1 cup / 200 ml
Green chillies, slit, deseeded	2 cups / 400 gm
Garlic (*lasan*) cloves, ground to paste	2
Turmeric (*haldi*) powder	1 tsp / 5 gm
Lemon (*nimbu*) juice	2 tbsp / 30 ml
Green coriander (*hara dhaniya*), chopped	¼ cup / 50 gm

Method:

1. Marinate the lamb with yoghurt, salt and cumin seeds. Keep aside for an hour.
2. Heat the oil in a heavy-bottomed pan; add the onions and fry to a golden brown.
3. Add the marinated lamb and water. Cook covered on a low flame, stirring occasionally.
4. When the lamb is almost done, add the green chillies, garlic paste and turmeric powder.
5. Cook till the lamb is tender and dry.
6. Add the lemon juice, garnish with green coriander and serve.

Khade Masale Ka Maas
Lamb cooked with whole spices

Preparation time: 30 min.
Cooking time: 1 hr. 15 min.
Serves: 4-6

Ingredients:

Lamb, cut into pieces	1 kg
Oil	1 cup / 200 ml
Black cardamoms (*badi elaichi*)	6
Cloves (*laung*)	6-8
Black peppercorns (*sabut kali mirch*)	1 tbsp / 15 gm
Cinnamon (*dalchini*) sticks	3-4
Bayleaves (*tej patta*)	5-6
Onions, finely sliced	3
Salt to taste	
Coriander seeds (*sabut dhaniya*)	1½ tbsp / 25 gm
Cumin seeds (*jeera*)	1 tsp / 5 gm
Whole red chillies (*sabut lal mirch*)	10
Ginger (*adrak*), 3" piece, julienned	1
Garlic (*lasan*), whole pods	8
Yoghurt (*dahi*)	1 cup / 200 gm

Method:

1. Heat the oil; add the spices from black cardamoms to bayleaves and onions. Fry till the onions are translucent.

2. Add the remaining ingredients and the lamb. Cook covered on a low flame, stirring occasionally.

3. When the lamb is nearly done, add the yoghurt and mix well. Simmer till the lamb is fully done and the oil separates. Serve hot.

Lamb

Laal Maas
Red, hot lamb curry

Preparation time: 30 min.
Cooking time: 1 hr. 15 min.
Serves: 4-6

Lamb

Ingredients:

Lamb, cut into pieces	1 kg
Oil	1½ cups / 300 ml
Red chilli powder	6 tsp / 30 gm
Coriander (*dhaniya*) powder	¼ cup / 50 gm
Onions, sliced	3
Yoghurt (*dahi*)	1¼ cups / 250 gm
Salt to taste	
Turmeric (*haldi*) powder	1 tsp / 5 gm
Garlic (*lasan*) paste	2 tbsp / 30 gm
Water, lukewarm	2 cups / 400 ml
Green coriander (*hara dhaniya*), chopped	1 tbsp / 15 gm

Photograph on page 2

Method:

1. Mix together all the ingredients (except garlic paste) and marinate the lamb pieces for one hour.
2. Heat the oil in a heavy-bottomed pan; add the lamb pieces and cook for 45 minutes on a slow fire till the pieces become tender.
3. Add the garlic paste and cook till the oil separates.
4. Add the water and bring to a boil. Garnish with green coriander and serve with hot *bajra* rotis (see p. 56).

Junglee Maas
No-fuss lamb recipe

Preparation time: 5 min.
Cooking time: I hr. I5 min.
Serves: 4-6

Ingredients:

Lamb, cut into pieces	1 kg
Oil	1½ cups / 300 ml
Salt to taste	
Water	½ cup / 100 ml
Red chilli powder	4-5 tbsp / 60-75 gm

Method:

1. Heat the oil in a heavy-bottomed deep pot. Add the lamb, salt and water.
2. Cook covered on a high flame, till it is heated through.
3. Lower the flame and cook for 30 minutes; making sure that the lamb does not stick to the bottom of the pot. Add the red chilli powder and cook till the lamb is tender.
4. Serve hot.

Kadhai Maas
Boneless lamb cooked with tomatoes

Preparation time: 15 min.
Cooking time: 1 hr. 15 min.
Serves: 4-6

Ingredients:

Lamb, boneless pieces	1 kg
Oil	1¼ cups / 250 ml
Tomatoes, red, pulpy	1 kg
Water	2-3 tbsp / 30-45 ml
Salt to taste	
Green chillies, large, cut into ¾" pieces	1¼ cups / 250 gm

Method:

1. Heat the oil in a wok (*kadhai*).
2. Blend the tomatoes and add to the wok (*kadhai*). Cook till the oil separates, stirring continuously.
3. Add the lamb and cook till it is almost tender, stirring and adding little water occasionally to prevent it from sticking to the bottom.
4. When the lamb is almost tender, add the salt and green chillies.
5. Cook till the green chillies are soft and the lamb is dry.
6. Serve hot.

Lamb

Sabut Murgh
Dry whole chicken

Preparation time: 30 min.
Cooking time: 45 min.
Serves: 4-6

Ingredients:

Chicken, medium-sized, cleaned	1
Oil	¾ cup / 150 ml
Onions, finely sliced	2
Garlic (*lasan*) pods, ground to paste	1½ tsp / 8 gm
Ginger (*adrak*), 2" piece, ground to paste	1
Red chilli powder	4 tsp / 20 gm
Coriander (*dhaniya*) powder	4 tsp / 20 gm
Salt to taste	
Turmeric (*haldi*) powder	½ tsp / 3 gm

Method:

1. Prick the chicken all over with a fork.
2. Heat the oil; fry the onions till they become brown.
3. Add the ginger-garlic pastes and fry till the oil separates.
4. Add all the dry spices and the chicken. Stir-fry the chicken for a few minutes.
5. Cook covered on a low flame, till the chicken is fully done. Add a little water if needed, to avoid the chicken from sticking to the bottom of the pan.
6. Once the chicken is done, then cook uncovered to dry the excess liquid. Serve hot.

Degchi Soola Murgh

Smoked chicken

Preparation time: 1 ½ hr.
Cooking time: ½ hr.
Serves: 2-4

Ingredients:

Chicken, cut into pieces	1 kg
Yoghurt (*dahi*), beaten	1¼ cups / 250 gm
Salt to taste	
Kachri powder (see p. 9)	2 tbsp / 30 gm
Garlic (*lasan*) paste	4 tbsp / 60 gm
Red chilli powder	3 tbsp / 45 gm
Oil	1¼ cups / 250 ml
Water	2-3 tbsp / 30-45 ml

Method:

1. Marinate the chicken with yoghurt, *kachri* powder and salt. Keep aside for 1-2 hours.
2. Mix together the chicken, garlic paste, red chilli powder and oil. Transfer to a pan and cook over a low flame adding water gradually at intervals, till the chicken becomes tender.
3. Transfer to a heat-proof dish. Smoke (see p. 93) with clarified butter and cloves for a few minutes and then serve immediately.

Murgh Ki Mokul
Spicy shredded chicken

Preparation time: 45 min.
Cooking time: 45 min.
Serves: 4-6

Ingredients:

Chicken, cut into pieces	1 kg
Clarified butter (*ghee*)	1¼ cups / 250 gm
Onions, large, chopped	4
Ginger (*adrak*), ground	1 tsp / 5 gm
Garlic (*lasan*), ground	1 tsp / 5 gm
Cumin seeds (*jeera*), ground	1 tsp / 5 gm
Red chilli powder	2 tsp / 10 gm
Coriander (*dhaniya*) powder	2 tsp / 10 gm
Yoghurt (*dahi*)	1¼ cups / 250 gm
Almonds (*badam*), blanched, ground	10
Coconut (*nariyal*), desiccated	1 tbsp / 15 gm
Salt to taste	
Green cardamoms (*choti elaichi*), powdered	½ tsp / 3 gm
Green chillies, slit	4
Green coriander (*hara dhaniya*), chopped	1 tbsp / 15 gm
Rose water (*gulabjal*)	1 tbsp / 15 ml

Method:

1. Boil the chicken for 15 minutes and keep aside to cool. Debone and shred it. Keep aside.
2. Heat the clarified butter; fry the onions till light brown. Add ingredients from ginger to coriander powder. Cook till the oil separates, stirring briskly.
3. Add the yoghurt, almonds, coconut and chicken. Cook on a low flame, until the gravy thickens.
4. Mix in the salt and cardamom powder. Garnish with green coriander and green chillies; add rose water just before serving.

Daal-Bati-Choorma
Pulses-bread-dessert delight

Preparation time: 1½ hr.
Cooking time: 1 hr.
Serves: 2-4

Panchmela daal

Ingredients:

Black gram (*urad dal*)	¼ cup / 50 gm
Bengal gram (*chana dal*)	¼ cup / 50 gm
Green gram (*moong dal*)	¼ cup / 50 gm
Red gram (*arhar dal*)	¼ cup / 50 gm
Lentil (*masur dal*)	¼ cup / 50 gm
Salt to taste	
Turmeric (*haldi*) powder	½ tsp / 3 gm
Water	1¼ cups / 250 ml
Clarified butter (*ghee*)	5 tbsp / 75 gm
Asafoetida (*hing*)	a pinch
Cumin seeds (*jeera*)	½ tsp / 3 gm
Cloves (*laung*)	5
Onions, chopped	2
Ginger-garlic (*adrak-lasan*) paste	2 tbsp / 30 gm
Red chilli powder	1 tsp / 5 gm
Ginger (*adrak*), chopped	2 tsp / 10 gm
Green chillies, chopped	1 tsp / 5 gm
Tomatoes, medium, chopped	3
Green coriander (*hara dhaniya*), chopped	1 tbsp / 15 gm
Ginger (*adrak*), julienned	1 tbsp / 15 gm
Green chillies, julienned	4

Method:

1. Mix the pulses, wash well, soak for half an hour.
2. Cook the pulses with salt, turmeric powder, and just enough water until tender.
3. Heat the clarified butter in a wok (*kadhai*). Add the asafoetida, cumin seeds and cloves. Sauté over a

Vegetarian

medium flame for a few seconds. Add the onions and sauté till golden brown.

4. Add ginger-garlic paste and red chilli powder. Cook for 3-4 minutes.
5. Add the ginger, green chillies and tomatoes and cook till the mixture leaves the sides of the pan.
6. Add the boiled pulses, mix well and heat through. Serve hot after garnishing with green coriander, ginger and green chillies.

Bati (*makes 14-16 pieces*)

Ingredients:

Flour (*maida*), sieved   2½ cups / 500 gm
Salt to taste

Ginger (*adrak*) paste   1 tbsp / 15 gm
Garlic (*lasan*) paste   1 tbsp / 15 gm
Green chillies, ground to paste   3
Clarified butter (*ghee*)   2½ cups / 500 gm

Method:

1. To the flour add salt, ginger-garlic paste, green chilli paste and 4 tbsp of clarified butter. Add just enough water to knead into a semi-hard dough.
2. Divide the dough into balls of 2″ diameter, to fit the hollow of the palm.
3. Place on a greased tray and bake in a moderately hot oven for 10 minutes. Change sides and bake again for 10 minutes. They should be lightly browned with a few cracks when done.
4. Remove and dip in melted clarified butter. Serve hot.

Choorma

Ingredients:

Batis (see p. 28) without ginger-garlic	10
Sugar, powdered	1 cup / 200 gm
Clarified butter (*ghee*)	1¼ cups / 250 gm
Green cardamoms (*choti elaichi*), powdered	8
Almonds (*badam*), blanched	12

Method:

1. Dip the *batis* liberally in melted clarified butter. Keep aside for 5 minutes to cool.
2. Crush them coarsely; add the sugar, 2 tbsp of clarified butter and the green cardamoms. Mix well.
3. To serve, either serve as a crushed mixture or roll into round balls which fit in the palm of the hand, garnished with slivers of almonds.

Forever Flour!
To retain the freshness of flour for months,
store it in dry polythene bags and
keep the bags in the fridge.

Kande Ki Sabzi
Spicy onions

Preparation time: 15 min.
Cooking time: 20 min.
Serves: 2-4

Vegetarian

Ingredients:

Onions, cut into big pieces	½ kg
Oil	½ cup / 100 ml
Cumin seeds (*jeera*)	1 tsp / 5 gm
Garlic (*lasan*) paste	1½ tsp / 8 gm
Ginger (*adrak*) paste	1½ tsp / 8 gm
Red chilli powder	1 tsp / 5 gm
Coriander (*dhaniya*) powder	2 tsp / 10 gm
Turmeric (*haldi*) powder	½ tsp / 3 gm
Salt to taste	
Water	1 cup / 200 ml
Yoghurt (*dahi*)	¼ cup / 50 gm

Method:

1. Heat the oil in a wok (*kadhai*). Sauté the cumin seeds for a few seconds.
2. Add the ginger and garlic pastes and fry till well browned.
3. Mix the dry spices in ½ cup of water and yoghurt. Add this to the wok (*kadhai*) and fry well.
4. When the mixture leaves the sides of the pan, add the onions and stir well.
5. Add ½ cup of water and cook on a low flame till the onions are tender but do not lose shape. Serve hot with *bajre ki roti* or *missi roti* (see p. 56).

Malai Paneer
Creamy cottage cheese

Preparation time: 20 min.
Cooking time: 30 min.
Serves: 2-4

Ingredients:

Cottage cheese (*paneer*), cut into cubes	3 cups / 600 gm
Oil	½ cup / 100 ml
Onions, medium, chopped	2
Ginger (*adrak*) paste	2 tbsp / 30 gm
Garlic (*lasan*) paste	2 tbsp / 30 gm
Red chilli powder	1 tsp / 5 gm
Coriander (*dhaniya*) powder	1 tbsp / 15 gm
Turmeric (*haldi*) powder	½ tsp / 3 gm
Salt to taste	
Cream (*malai*)	½ cup / 100 ml

Method:

1. Heat the oil in a wok (*kadhai*). Add the onions and fry till they are golden brown.
2. Mix the ginger and garlic pastes, the red chilli powder, coriander powder, turmeric powder and salt together. Add to the wok (*kadhai*) and cook for 4-5 minutes.
3. Add the cottage cheese cubes and stir till they are evenly coated with the spice mixture.
4. Add the cream and stir well for 2 minutes or till the oil separates. Remove from the flame and serve hot.

Hare Tamatar Ki Sabzi

Spicy green tomatoes

Preparation time: 15 min.
Cooking time: 20 min.
Serves: 2-4

Vegetarian

Ingredients:

Green tomatoes, cut into big pieces	½ kg
Oil	¼ cup / 50 ml
Cumin seeds (*jeera*)	½ tsp / 3 gm
Fenugreek seeds (*methi dana*)	½ tsp / 3 gm
Green chillies, slit	2-3
Red chilli powder	1 tsp / 5 gm
Coriander (*dhaniya*) powder	2 tsp / 10 gm
Turmeric (*haldi*) powder	½ tsp / 3 gm
Salt to taste	
Mango powder (*amchur*)	½ tsp / 3 gm
Sugar	a pinch
Garlic (*lasan*) paste	1 tsp / 5 gm

Method:

1. Heat the oil in a wok (*kadhai*). Sauté the cumin and fenugreek seeds, when they crackle, add the tomatoes and green chillies. Fry for 1-2 minutes.
2. Add all the dry spices and sugar. Cook covered for 5-6 minutes, or till the tomato slices lose their shape.
3. Add the garlic paste and stir-fry for 2-3 minutes.
4. Serve hot with *missi* roti (see p. 56) and a glass of *chaach* (see p. 60).

Ker Sangri
A desert speciality

Preparation time: 20 min.
Cooking time: 45 min.
Serves: 2-4

Ingredients:

Sangri (see p. 9), dried	1 cup / 200 gm
Ker (see p. 9), dried	¼ cup / 50 gm
Yoghurt (*dahi*)	1 cup / 200 gm
Water	2½ cups / 500 ml
Oil	¾ cup / 150 ml
Onions, medium, chopped	2
Red chilli powder	2 tsp / 10 gm
Coriander (*dhaniya*) powder	3 tbsp / 45 gm
Turmeric (*haldi*) powder	½ tsp / 3 gm
Salt to taste	
Garlic (*lasan*) paste	2 tbsp / 30 gm

Method:

1. Soak the *ker* in ½ cup of yoghurt and 2 cups of water for 10 hours.
2. Wash the *sangri* 2-3 times in running water.
3. Pressure cook the *ker* and *sangri* for 10-15 minutes.
4. Drain out the water and transfer the *ker* and *sangri* to a wok (*kadhai*). Add all the ingredients (except the garlic paste).
5. Cover and cook on a low flame for 30-45 minutes or till the oil separates.
6. Add the garlic paste and stir till all the water dries.
7. Add ½ cup of warm water and bring to a boil. Simmer for another 5 minutes. Serve hot with *bajre ki* roti (see p. 56).

Makki Ki Sabzi
Spicy corn

Preparation time: 20 min.
Cooking time: 30 min.
Serves: 2-4

Ingredients:

Corn (*makkai*) kernels, coarsely grated	½ kg
Oil	5 tbsp / 75 ml
Cumin seeds (*jeera*)	½ tsp / 3 gm
Onion, finely chopped	1
Ginger (*adrak*) paste	1½ tsp / 8 gm
Garlic (*lasan*) paste	1½ tsp / 8 gm
Turmeric (*haldi*) powder	½ tsp / 3 gm
Salt to taste	
Red chilli powder	½ tsp / 3 gm
Coriander (*dhaniya*) powder	1 tsp / 5 gm
Water	2½ cups / 500 ml
Cream (*malai*), whipped	½ cup / 100 ml
Green coriander (*hara dhaniya*), chopped	1 tbsp / 15 gm

Method:

1. Heat the oil; add the cumin seeds and onions and sauté till the onions are golden brown. Add the ginger and garlic pastes. Cook until brown.
2. Mix the turmeric powder, salt, red chilli powder and coriander powder in ½ cup of water. Add to the pan and cook for 5 minutes on a low flame.
3. When the mixture leaves the sides of the pan, add the corn and fry for 5 minutes.
4. Add 2 cups of water, cover and cook on a low flame for 10-12 minutes.
5. When the corn is tender and the liquid has almost dried, mix in the cream.
6. Garnish with green coriander and serve.

Besan Ki Hari Mirch

Green chillies stuffed with gram flour

Preparation time: 15 min.
Cooking time: 30 min.
Serves: 2-4

Ingredients:

Green chillies, large, slit	½ kg
Gram flour (*besan*)	½ cup / 100 gm
Salt to taste	
Red chilli powder	½ tsp / 3 gm
Turmeric (*haldi*) powder	¼ tsp / 1½ gm
Coriander (*dhaniya*) powder	½ tsp / 3 gm
Mango powder (*amchur*)	1 tsp / 5 gm
Water	¼ cup / 50 ml
Oil	½ cup / 100 ml

Method:

1. Roast the gram flour in a wok (*kadhai*) for 5 minutes till it emanates a roasted fragrance.
2. Add all the dry spices along with water and cook till a thick paste-like consistency is obtained. Stir continuously. Remove from the flame and put aside to cool.
3. Stuff the green chillies with the gram flour paste.
4. Heat the oil and fry the green chillies, uncovered on a low flame till they become tender and change colour. Remove from the flame and serve hot.

Pithore

Gram flour pieces in spicy yoghurt curry

Preparation time: 20 min.
Cooking time: I hr.
Serves: 4-6

Ingredients:

For the *pithore*

Gram flour (*besan*)	1¼ cups / 250 gm
Yoghurt (*dahi*)	2½ cups / ½ kg
Ginger-garlic (*adrak-lasan*) paste	2 tbsp / 30 gm
Red chilli powder	1 tsp / 5 gm
Turmeric (*haldi*) powder	½ tsp / 3 gm
Salt to taste	
Green coriander (*hara dhaniya*), chopped	a few sprigs
Ginger (*adrak*), 1" piece, chopped	1
Green chillies, chopped	2
Water	1½ cups / 250 ml
Oil	¾ cup / 150 ml

For dry *pithore*

Oil	3 tbsp / 45 ml
Mustard seeds (*rai*)	1 tsp / 5 gm
Lemon (*nimbu*), juice	1

For gravied *pithore*

Oil	½ cup / 100 ml
Cloves (*laung*)	3
Black cardamoms (*badi elaichi*)	2
Cinammon (*dalchini*) sticks, small	2
Onions, finely chopped	2
Ginger-garlic (*adrak-lasan*) paste	4 tsp / 20 gm
Red chilli powder	1 tsp / 5 gm
Turmeric (*haldi*) powder	½ tsp / 3 gm
Salt to taste	
Coriander (*dhaniya*) powder	2 tbsp / 30 gm
Yoghurt (*dahi*)	½ cup / 100 gm
Water	1 cup / 200 ml

Vegetarian

Method:

1. **For the *pithore***, mix together the gram flour, yoghurt, ginger-garlic paste, red chilli powder, turmeric powder, salt, green coriander, ginger and green chillies. Add water and mix well.
2. Heat the oil in a wok (*kadhai*). Gradually pour the above mixture into the wok (*kadhai*). Cook till the mixture leaves the sides of the wok (*kadhai*).
3. Spread the mixture uniformly in a greased tray. Let it set for 1-2 hours.
4. Cut with a knife into 1″ cubes or diamond shapes.
5. **For serving dry *pithore***, heat the oil in a wok (*kadhai*). Add the mustard seeds; when they crackle, add the *pithore* pieces. Stir gently for a minute. Remove from the flame and arrange in a dish.
6. Sprinkle the juice of a lemon on top, garnish with green coriander and serve as a snack.
7. **For serving gravied *pithore***, heat the oil in a wok (*kadhai*). Add the cloves, black cardamoms and cinnamon sticks. Sauté over medium heat for a few seconds.
8. Add the onions and cook till they are golden brown in colour.
9. Mix the ginger-garlic paste, red chilli powder, turmeric powder, salt and coriander powder with the yoghurt. Add this to the wok (*kadhai*).
10. Cook till the oil separates. Add the *pithore* pieces and the water. Bring to a boil and then simmer for 5 minutes. Serve hot.

Gatte Ka Saag

Steamed gram flour dumplings in spicy gravy

Preparation time: 15 min.
Cooking time: 45 min.
Serves: 2-4

I n g r e d i e n t s :

Gram flour (*besan*)	1¼ cups / 250 gm
Yoghurt (*dahi*), sour	2 cups / 400 gm
Salt to taste	
Red chilli powder	2 tsp / 10 gm
Turmeric (*haldi*) powder	1 tsp / 5 gm
Oil	1 cup / 200 ml
Water to boil	
Cumin seeds (*jeera*)	3 tsp / 15 gm
Water	1 cup / 200 ml
Coriander (*dhaniya*) powder	1 tbsp / 15 gm

M e t h o d :

1. Make a soft dough with the gram flour, ½ cup yoghurt, ¾ tsp salt, 3 tbsp oil, ¾ tsp red chilli powder and ½ tsp turmeric powder.

2. Apply a little oil on the hands and roll out 1"x 6" long cylindrical rolls of the dough.

3. Bring the water to a boil and slide in the rolls. Cook for 5-7 minutes or till they become firm. Drain the water and put the rolls aside to cool for 15 minutes. Cut into ¾"-long pieces.

4. Heat the remaining oil; add the cumin seeds and let them crackle. Add the gram flour pieces and stir-fry for 1-2 minutes.

5. To the remaining yoghurt, add the leftover spices and mix well. Add this mixture to the pieces, stir and cook for 2-3 minutes. Add salt to taste.

6. Add water and bring to a boil. Simmer for 5-7 minutes. If the gravy is very thick, add a little more water and boil till the oil separates. Serve hot.

Papad Ki Sabzi

Sun-dried wafers in curry

Preparation time: 15 min.
Cooking time: 20 min.
Serves: 2-4

Vegetarian

Ingredients:

Wafers (*papad*), see p. 9	4 / 5
Oil	4-5 tbsp / 60-75 ml
Cumin seeds (*jeera*)	½ tsp / 3 gm
Onions, finely chopped	2
Kachri (see p. 9), ground	1 tbsp / 15 gm
Garlic (*lasan*), ground	2 cloves
Red chilli powder	2 tsp / 10 gm
Coriander (*dhaniya*) powder	2 tbsp / 30 gm
Turmeric (*haldi*) powder	½ tsp / 3 gm
Yoghurt (*dahi*)	3 tbsp / 45 gm

Method:

1. Heat the oil in a wok (*kadhai*). Add the cumin seeds and onions. Fry till the onions get brown.
2. Mix all the dry spices in yoghurt with 2-3 tbsp of water. Add the mixture to the fried onions. Stir till the oil separates.
3. Break the wafers into small triangular pieces and add to the yoghurt mixture.
4. Add just enough water to immerse the wafers.
5. Cook for 10 minutes or till the wafers become tender.

Kadhi
Gram flour curry

Preparation time: 15 min.
Cooking time: 20 min.
Serves: 2-4

Ingredients:

Green coriander (*hara dhaniya*),
chopped   1 tbsp / 15 gm

Gram flour (*besan*)	3 tbsp / 45 gm
Oil	2 tbsp / 30 ml
Asafoetida (*hing*)	¼ tsp / 1½ gm
Mustard seeds (*rai*)	½ tsp / 3 gm
Cumin seeds (*jeera*)	½ tsp / 3 gm
Onion, big, chopped	1
Yoghurt (*dahi*), sour	1¼ cups / 250 gm
Garlic (*lasan*) paste	1 tbsp / 15 gm
Green chillies, ground to paste	2
Red chilli powder	¼ tsp / 1½ gm
Turmeric (*haldi*) powder	¼ tsp / 1½ gm
Salt to taste	
Water	2 cups / 400 ml
Curry leaves (*kadhi patta*)	a few sprigs

Method:

1. Heat the oil in a wok (*kadhai*). Add the asafoetida, mustard seeds and cumin seeds.
2. When they crackle, add the onion and fry till the onion browns.
3. Whisk the yoghurt with the garlic paste, green chilli paste, red chilli powder, turmeric powder, gram flour and salt. Add water and stir.
4. Add to the wok (*kadhai*) and bring to a boil. Add the curry leaves and then simmer for 10 minutes.
5. Garnish with green coriander. Serve with rotis or plain boiled rice.

Bajre Ka Soyta
Millet and lamb porridge

Preparation time: 1 hr.
Cooking time: 2½-3 hr.
Serves: 4-6

Ingredients:

Lamb	½ kg
Millet grains (*bajra*)	½ kg
Salt to taste	
Water	6 cups / 1.2 lt
Clarified butter (*ghee*)	¾ cup / 150 gm
Red chilli powder	¼ cup / 50 gm
Coriander (*dhaniya*) powder	6 tsp / 30 gm
Turmeric (*haldi*) powder	1 tsp / 5 gm
Onions, medium, sliced	4
Ginger (*adrak*), ground, 3″ piece	1
Garlic (*lasan*) pods, large, ground	2-3
Green chillies	15-20
Green coriander (*hara dhaniya*)	2 tbsp / 30 gm
Ginger (*adrak*), julienned	1 tbsp / 15 gm
Red chillies, deseeded, fried	4-5

Method:

1. Sprinkle a little water on the millet grains and put aside for 30 minutes. Pound lightly to split the grains. Pass through a sieve to remove the chaf.
2. Boil the lamb with salt and 1 cup of water till it is half done.
3. Heat the clarified butter in a pan; add all the dry spices along with the millet. Sauté for a while. Add the onion, ginger, garlic, the lamb and green chillies. Mix well.
4. Add the remaining water; let it cook on a low flame till the lamb is tender and the water is absorbed.
5. Garnish with chopped green coriander, ginger and red chilli shells. Serve hot.

Mangodi Pulao

Fried rice with green gram dumplings

Preparation time: 15 min.
Cooking time: 25 min.
Serves: 4-6

Accompaniments

Ingredients:

Basmati rice	3 cups / 600 gm
Mangodi (see p. 9)	1 cup / 200 gm
Oil	1 cup / 200 ml
Green cardamoms (*choti elaichi*)	5
Black cardamoms (*badi elaichi*)	2
Cloves (*laung*)	5
Cinnamon (*dalchini*) sticks	2
Bayleaves (*tej patta*)	2
Cumin seeds (*jeera*)	½ tsp / 3 gm
Salt to taste	
Water	7 cups / 1½ lt
Onion, sliced, browned	1

Method:

1. Soak the rice for 10 minutes.
2. Heat 2 tbsp of oil in a wok (*kadhai*). Shallow fry the *mangodis* on medium flame for 2-3 minutes. Drain the excess oil and keep aside.
3. Heat the remaining oil in a pan. Add the green cardamons, black cardamoms, cloves, cinnamon sticks, bayleaves and cumin seeds. Sauté over a medium flame till the seeds crackle.
4. Add the rice (drained) and *mangodis*. Stir gently, add the salt and water.
5. Bring to a boil and then lower the flame. Cook until the liquid dries, stirring only occasionally, very gently.
6. Garnish with browned onion slices and serve.

Masala Batis

Unleavened bread

Preparation time: 15 min.
Cooking time: 3 min. each
Serves: 4-6

Ingredients:

Bati dough (as per recipe on p. 28)	
Green peas (*mattar*)	¾ cup / 150 gm
Oil	4 tbsp / 60 ml
Cumin seeds (*jeera*)	½ tsp / 3 gm
Onion, medium, chopped	1
Coriander (*dhaniya*) powder	1 tsp / 5 gm
Red chilli powder	½ tsp / 3 gm
Green chillies, chopped	1 tsp / 5 gm
Tomato, medium, chopped	1
Green coriander (*hara dhaniya*), chopped	2 tbsp / 30 gm

Method:

1. Heat the oil in a wok (*kadhai*). Add the cumin seeds; when they crackle, add the onion and sauté till it is well browned.

2. Add the coriander powder, red chilli powder, green chillies and tomato. Cook till the tomato becomes soft.

3. Add the green peas. Lower the flame and cook till they become tender and the excess liquid dries. Garnish with green coriander.

4. When the mixture cools, fill small portions of it in the *batis* (see recipe for *batis* on page 28) and bake in an oven, as mentioned.
   Note: For non-vegetarian batis, use lamb mince instead of green peas.

Missi Roti
Mixed flour unleavened bread

Prep. time: 15 min. Cooking time: 3 min. Serves: 4

Ingredients:

Wheat flour (*gehu ka atta*)	1 cup / 200 gm
Bengal gram flour (*kale chane ka atta*)	1 cup / 200 gm
Salt and red chilli powder to taste	
Oil	2 tbsp / 30 gm
Clarified butter (*ghee*) to smear	

Method:

1. Mix all the ingredients (except clarified butter); knead into a soft dough by adding adequate water. Separate into small balls; roll each into flat rounds 6-8" in diameter.
2. Heat a griddle (*tawa*) and roast each round evenly on both sides. Smear one side with a little clarified butter and serve.

Bajre Ki Roti
Millet flour unleavened bread

Prep. time: 15 min. Cooking time: 3 min. Serves: 4

Ingredients:

Millet flour (*bajre ka atta*)	1½ cups / 300 gm
Wheat flour (*gehu ka atta*)	½ cup / 100 gm
Clarified butter (*ghee*) to smear	

Method:

1. Mix the two flours together and knead into a soft dough by adding adequate water.
2. Separate the dough into small balls and then roll each into flat rounds 6-8" in diameter.
3. Heat a griddle (*tawa*) and roast each round evenly on both sides. Remove from the pan; smear one side with a little clarified butter and serve.

Methi Ki Roti

Fenugreek-wheat flour unleavened bread

Preparation time: 15 min.
Cooking time: 3 min. each
Serves: 4-6

Ingredients:

Wheat flour (*gehu ka atta*)	2 cups / 400 gm
Fenugreek leaves (*methi*), finely chopped	1½ cups / 300 gm
Salt to taste	
Red chilli powder	1 tsp / 5 gm
Clarified butter (*ghee*)	½ cup / 100 gm

Method:

1. Mix all the ingredients together (except clarified butter).
2. Knead into a soft dough by adding adequate water.
3. Separate the dough into small balls and then roll each into flat rounds 6-8" in diameter.
4. Heat a griddle (*tawa*) and roast each round evenly on both sides. Remove from the pan, smear one side with a little clarified butter and serve.

*(Photograph on page 57, **top:** Missi Roti; **centre:** Bajre ki Roti; **bottom:** Methi ki Roti.)*

Aam Ka Panna

Tangy mango drink

Preparation time: 45 min.
Cooking time: 30 min.
Serves: 2-4

Ingredients:

Mangoes, raw, peeled, sliced	¾ kg
Water	5 cups / 1 lt
Salt to taste	
Sugar	10 tbsp / 150 gm
Cumin seeds (*jeera*), powdered	1 tsp / 5 gm
Mint leaves (*pudina*), finely chopped	one bunch

Method:

1. Cook the mangoes with the water for half an hour. Remove from the flame.
2. Mash the mango pieces to pulp and pass the mixture through a sieve.
3. Mix in the salt, sugar and cumin seed powder. Stir well till the sugar dissolves.
4. Serve chilled, garnished with mint leaves.

*(Photograph on page 61, **left:** Amalvaniya; **centre:** Chaach; **right:** Aam ka Panna.)*

Chaach
Flavoured buttermilk

Preparation time: 15 min.   Serves: 2-4

Ingredients:

Yoghurt (*dahi*)	2½ cups / ½ kg
Water	5 cups / 1 lt
Salt to taste	
Cumin seeds (*jeera*), powdered, roasted	1 tsp / 5 gm
Mint leaves (*pudina*) dried, crushed	1 tsp / 5 gm

Method:

1. Whisk the yoghurt well.
2. Add the water, salt and cumin seed powder. Mix well.
3. Garnish with mint leaves and serve chilled.

Amalvaniya
Sweet and sour tamarind drink

Preparation time: 45 min.   Serves: 2-4

Ingredients:

Tamarind (*imli*)	1 cup / 200 gm
Water	5 cups / 1 lt
Sugar	1 cup / 200 gm

Method:

1. Soak the tamarind in 1 cup of warm water. Extract the pulp.
2. Add the remaining water and sugar. Stir till the sugar dissolves completely.
3. Pass the mixture through a sieve. Serve chilled.

Rabadi
Millet flour in yoghurt

Preparation time: 15 min.
Cooking time: 3 hr.
Serves: 4-6

Ingredients:

Yoghurt (*dahi*)	1¼ cups / 250 gm
Millet flour (*bajra*)	4 tbsp / 60 gm
Butter	7 tsp / 35 gm
Ginger-garlic (*adrak-lasan*) paste	4 tsp / 20 gm
Water	15 cups / 3 lt
Salt to taste	
Cumin seeds (*jeera*), powdered, roasted	1 tsp / 5 gm
Green coriander (*hara dhaniya*), chopped	1 tbsp / 15 gm

Method:

1. Mix together the yoghurt and the flour in a bowl. Keep aside.
2. Heat the butter in a pot. Add the ginger-garlic paste and sauté over medium heat for 2-3 minutes or until brown in colour.
3. Stir in the flour-yoghurt mixture and bring to a boil.
4. Add water and let it simmer, till it is reduced to two-third the original quantity.
5. Add salt and mix well. Remove from the fire and cool to room temperature. Pass the mixture through a muslin cloth. Serve chilled, garnished with cumin seed powder and green coriander.

Dhungar Ka Pyaz
Smoked onions

Ingredients:

Onions, sliced	4
Salt to taste	
Green chillies, chopped	2
Lemon (*nimbu*), juice	1 tbsp / 15 ml

Method:

1. Mix salt, green chillies and lemon juice with the onions.
2. Arrange the onions on a salad platter. Leave space in the middle to put the smoking material.
3. Smoke (see p. 93) with clarified butter for 10 minutes and then serve.

Photograph on page 4

Machchi Ka Achar
Fish pickle

Ingredients:

Fish, big, cut into 1½" cubes	1 kg
Garlic (*lasan*)	2 pods
Ginger (*adrak*), cut into 1" pieces	3
Cumin seeds (*jeera*)	5 tsp / 25 gm
Black peppercorns (*sabut kali mirch*)	3 tsp / 15 gm
Red chilli powder	3 tsp / 15 gm
Vinegar (*sirka*)	6 tbsp / 90 ml
Oil	1¾ cups / 350 ml
Turmeric (*haldi*) powder	1 tsp / 5 gm
Green chillies, slit	8-10
Mustard seeds (*rai*)	1 tsp / 5 gm
Salt to taste	

Method:

1. Fry the fish pieces until crispy and brown. Break into smaller pieces and keep aside.
2. Grind to a paste, one pod of garlic, ginger, cumin seeds, black peppercorns, red chilli powder and 3 tbsp of vinegar.
3. Heat the oil in a wok (*kadhai*). Remove from the flame, cool and add the turmeric powder. Return to flame, add the ground paste. Fry till it browns. Add the fish, green chillies, mustard seeds and the remaining pod of garlic (slit). Cook for 5 minutes.
4. Remove from the flame and add the remaining vinegar and salt. After it cools store in airtight jars. Make sure the pickle is covered with oil. If not, then heat some oil, cool and then add to the pickle.

Maas Ka Achar
Venison Pickle

Preparation time: ½ hr.
Cooking time: 2 hr.

Ingredients:

Venison, cut into 1½" cubes	1kg
Oil	2 cups / 400 ml
Red chilli powder	4 tbsp / 60 gm
Turmeric (*haldi*) powder	2 tsp / 10 gm
Salt	3 tsp / 15 gm
Aniseed (*saunf*)	5 tsp / 25 gm
Cumin seeds (*jeera*)	5 tsp / 25 gm
Fenugreek seeds (*methi dana*)	2½ tbsp / 40 gm
Mustard seeds (*rai*)	10 tsp / 50 gm
Vinegar (*sirka*), white	1 cup / 200 ml

Method:

1. Heat the oil; add all the dry spices and the venison pieces.
2. Cook on a low flame till the venison becomes tender.
3. Remove from the flame. When it cools, add the vinegar and store in an airtight container.

*(Photograph on page 65, **left:** Machchi ka Achar; **right:** Maas ka Achar.)*

Kachri Ki Chutney

Tangy relish

Ingredients:

Kachri (see p. 9), ground   2 tbsp / 30 gm
Oil to fry
Cumin seeds (*jeera*), powdered   1 tsp / 5 gm
Garlic (*lasan*), ground   ½ cup / 100 gm
Onion, medium, chopped   1
Whole red chillies (*sabut lal*
  mirch), ground   2-3 tbsp / 30-45 gm
Yoghurt (*dahi*)   ½ cup / 100 gm
Salt to taste

Method:

1. Heat 1 tsp of oil; add the cumin seeds and garlic. Sauté for a few seconds.
2. Add the onion and fry till it browns.
3. Add the remaining ingredients and cook on a low flame till the oil separates. Store in an airtight jar. If refrigerated this chutney will stay for a month.

Lahsun Ki Chutney
Garlic chutney

Preparation time: 30 min.

Ingredients:

Garlic (*lasan*), skinned	½ cup / 100 gm
Cumin seeds (*jeera*)	1 tsp / 5 gm
Red chilli powder	2-3 tsp / 10-15 gm
Yoghurt (*dahi*)	¼ cup / 50 gm
Salt to taste	

Method:

1. Mix together all the ingredients.
2. Grind / blend to a smooth paste.
3. Store in an airtight jar until ready to use. If refrigerated, this chutney will easily stay for 2 weeks.

Dhaniya Ki Chutney
Coriander chutney

Preparation time: 15 min.

Ingredients:

Green coriander (*hara dhaniya*)	1 cup / 100 gm
Tomato, big	1
Onion, big	1
Green chillies	3-4
Salt to taste	
Lemon (*nimbu*), juice	1

Method:

1. Grind all ingredients (except salt and lemon juice) with just enough water to make a smooth paste.
2. Add salt and lemon juice and mix well.
3. Store, refrigerated in a clean dry jar.

Aam Ki Launj

Mango relish

Prep. time: 30 min.
Cooking time: 30 min.

Ingredients:

Mangoes, raw, unpeeled, pieces	700 gm
Mustard (*sarson*) oil	½ cup / 100 ml
Panch phoran (see p. 9)	1 tsp / 5 gm
Red chilli powder + salt to taste	
Turmeric (*haldi*) powder	½ tsp / 3 gm
Coriander (*dhaniya*) powder	1 ½ tsp / 8 gm
Water, Jaggery (*gur*)	150 ml, 150 gm

Method:

1. Heat the oil in a wok (*kadhai*); crackle the *panch phoran*. Add all the ingredients (except jaggery and water). Sprinkle 2-3 tbsp of water and cook covered for 5-7 minutes.
2. When the mangoes soften a little, add the jaggery and ½ cup of water. Cook till tender.

Tamater Ki Launj

Tomato relish

Prep. time: 15 min.
Cooking time: 15 min.

Ingredients:

Tomatoes, chopped	¾ kg
Oil	2 tbsp / 30 ml
Panch phoran (see p. 9)	1 tsp / 5 gm
Green chillies, slit	2
Red chilli powder + salt to taste	
Turmeric (*haldi*) powder	½ tsp / 3 gm
Coriander (*dhaniya*) powder	1 tsp / 5 gm
Sugar	4 tbsp / 20 gm

Method:

1. Heat the oil in a wok; crackle the *panch phoran*. Add all the ingredients, mix well and cook covered on a low flame for 7 minutes.
2. Add the sugar and cook till a gravy-like consistency is reached. Serve cold.

Pyaaz Ka Raita
Yoghurt flavoured with fried onions

Preparation time: 15 min.
Cooking time: 15 min.
Serves: 4-6

Ingredients:

Yoghurt (*dahi*), whisked	2½ cups / 500 gm
Water	½ cup / 100 ml
Salt to taste	
Oil	1 tbsp / 15 ml
Cumin seeds (*jeera*)	1 tsp / 5 gm
Onions, small, chopped	2
Red chilli powder	½ tsp / 3 gm
Turmeric (*haldi*) powder	¼ tsp / 1½ gm

Method:

1. Mix the water and 1 tsp salt into the yoghurt and keep aside.
2. Heat the oil in a wok (*kadhai*); add cumin seeds and let them crackle.
3. Add the onions and fry till they brown and then add the red chilli powder and turmeric powder. Remove from the flame.
4. Pour this mixture into the yoghurt and mix well.
5. Smoke (see p. 93) the *raita* with clarified butter.

Accompaniments

Kachumbar / Choori
Fresh salad

Ingredients:

Onions, small	2
Tomatoes	3
Capsicum (*Shimla mirch*)	1
Cucumber (*kheera*)	2
Salt to taste	
Green chillies, chopped	2
Green coriander (*hara dhaniya*)	1 tbsp / 15 gm
Lemon (*nimbu*), juice	1 tbsp / 15 ml

Method:

1. Dice the onions, tomatoes, capsicum and the cucumber into small ¼" cubes.
2. Add salt, green chillies, green coriander, and lemon juice.
3. Mix well and serve cold.

Maas Ke Sooley
Barbecued spicy lamb

Preparation time: 5 hr.
Cooking time: 30 min.
Serves: 2-4

Ingredients:

Lamb, boneless pieces	1 kg
Clarified butter (*ghee*) to baste	
For the 1st marination:	
Basil (*tulsi*), dried, crushed	1 tbsp / 15 gm
Raw papaya, ground to paste	½ cup / 100 gm
Garlic (*lasan*) paste	2 tbsp / 30 gm
Red chilli powder	3 tsp / 15 gm
Salt to taste	
Clarified butter (*ghee*)	1 cup / 200 gm
Onions, medium, peeled, sliced	2
Garlic (*lasan*) cloves, chopped	12
For the 2nd marination:	
Ginger (*adrak*), 1½" piece	1

Basil (*tulsi*), crushed	1 tbsp / 15 gm
Kachri powder (see p. 9)	2 tbsp / 30 gm
Cloves (*laung*), powdered	½ tsp / 3 gm
Black cardamoms (*badi elaichi*), powdered	2 tsp / 10 gm
Nutmeg (*jaiphal*), powdered	2 tsp / 10 gm
Cinnamon (*dalchini*) powder	a pinch
Yoghurt (*dahi*)	1½ cups / 300 gm
Soola masala (mix together)	
Mango powder (*amchur*)	1 tsp / 5 gm
Black rock salt powder	½ tsp / 3 gm
Black pepper powder (*kali mirch*)	½ tsp / 3 gm
Green cardamoms (*choti elaichi*), powdered	½ tsp / 3 gm
Nutmeg (*jaiphal*), powdered	¼ tsp / 1½ gm

Method:

1. Wash and pat dry the lamb pieces.
2. For the first marination, mix all the ingredients and evenly rub the mixture on the pieces. Keep aside for 2 hours.
3. Heat the clarified butter in a wok (*kadhai*) and deep-fry the onions and garlic separately over medium heat, until golden brown. Drain the excess oil on absorbent paper and keep aside.
4. For the second marination, blend together the ingredients for the second marinade (except yoghurt). Add 2 tbsp of water to make into a smooth paste. Remove to a bowl, add the yoghurt and whisk well.
5. Evenly rub the pieces with the second marinade and keep aside for 2 hours.
6. Skewer the pieces and roast for 12-15 minutes. Baste with clarified butter and roast again for 12-15 minutes or till the pieces are tender.
7. Smoke (see p. 93) for 2 minutes with cloves and clarified butter. Arrange on a platter, sprinkle *soola masala* and serve hot.

Flavoured Barbecue!

Sprinkle some lemon juice over the hot coals in the last few minutes of grilling to add flavour to the meat.

Venison Sooley

Barbecued spicy venison

Preparation time: 2½ hr.
Cooking time: 30 min.
Serves: 4-6

Ingredients:

Venison, boneless, cut into 1" pieces	1 kg
Red chilli powder	3 tbsp / 45 gm
Garlic (*lasan*) paste	3 tbsp / 45 gm
Kachri powder (see p. 9)	3 tbsp / 45 gm
Yoghurt (*dahi*)	1 cup / 200 gm
Salt to taste	
Onions, medium, whole, peeled	2
Onions, cut into rings	2

Method:

1. Mix all the ingredients and marinate the venison pieces for about 2 hours.

2. Skewer the venison tightly, placing the onions at the end. Roast over a rack with heated coal underneath for about 20-25 minutes or till the pieces are tender. Rotate the skewer at regular intervals.

3. Transfer the pieces to a pre-heated dish and smoke (see p. 93) the pieces with clarified butter and garlic paste. Arrange on a platter, sprinkle *soola masala* (see p. 76) and serve with the onion rings.

Murgh Ke Sooley

Barbecued chicken

Preparation time: 3 hr.
Cooking time: 20 min.
Serves: 2-4

Ingredients:

Chicken, boneless, cubes	1 kg
Salt to taste or	1 tsp / 5 gm
Ginger (*adrak*) paste	1 tbsp / 15 gm
Garlic (*lasan*) paste	1 tbsp / 15 gm
Kachri powder (see p. 9)	1 tbsp / 15 gm
Yoghurt (*dahi*), whisked	1 cup / 200 gm
Red chilli powder	1 tsp / 5 gm
Black peppercorns (*sabut kali mirch*), ground	1 tsp / 5 gm
Cumin seeds (*jeera*), powdered	1 tsp / 5 gm
Clarified butter (*ghee*) to baste	
Lemon (*nimbu*), juice	1½ tbsp / 25 ml
Onions, medium, cut into rings	2

Method:

1. Marinate the chicken with salt, ginger-garlic paste and *kachri* powder. Keep aside for 2-3 hours.
2. Add the yoghurt, red chilli powder, black pepper and cumin seed powders. Mix well together.
3. Skewer the chicken pieces and roast in a moderately hot oven for about 8-10 minutes or until almost cooked. Remove and hang the skewers for about 2-3 minutes to allow the excess marinade to drip. Baste with clarified butter and roast again for 2-3 minutes.
4. Smoke (see p. 93) with cloves and clarified butter for 2 minutes. Uncover and sprinkle *soola masala* (see p. 76). Squeeze the lemon juice, garnish with onion rings and serve.

Machchi Ki Tikki
Fish Cutlets

Preparation time: ½ hr.
Cooking time: 45 min.
Serves: 4-6

Ingredients:

Rohu fish, mashed	½ kg
Bread slices	2
Cumin seeds (*jeera*)	2 tsp / 10 gm
Black peppercorns (*sabut kali mirch*), ground	1 tsp / 5 gm
Onions, large, finely chopped	2
Green chillies, finely chopped	4-5
Dry fenugreek leaves (*kasoori methi*)	2 tbsp / 30 gm
Salt to taste	
Egg, beaten	1
Breadcrumbs	7 tbsp / 105 gm
Oil to fry	

Method:

1. Boil the fish in very little water. Debone the flesh.
2. Soak the bread in water and squeeze dry.
3. Add all the ingredients (up to the salt) to the mashed fish and mix well.
4. Shape into desired size cutlets. Dip the cutlets in egg, then coat well with breadcrumbs and shallow fry. Serve hot with *Dhaniya ki chutney* (see p. 68).

Moong Dal Ke Chille
Green gram pancakes

Preparation time: 3 hr.
Cooking time: 30 min.
Serves: 2-4

Ingredients:

Green gram (*moong dal*),
washed   1¼ cups / 250 gm

Ginger-garlic (*adrak-lasan*)
paste   2 tbsp / 30 gm

Green chillies, chopped   3

Green coriander (*hara dhaniya*),
chopped   1 tbsp / 15 gm

Salt to taste

Oil to fry

Method:

1. Soak the green gram for 2-3 hours. Drain and grind to a fine paste, adding a little water.
2. Add the remaining ingredients (except oil) and mix well.
3. Add a little more water to bring the mixture to a dropping consistency.
4. Smear 2 tsp of oil in a non-stick pan; pour 2 tbsp of the mixture in the pan and spread to form a flat round pancake. Cook over a low flame till both the sides are golden brown in colour. Fry 6-8 such round pancakes.
5. Serve hot with *Lahsun ki chutney* or *Dhaniya ki chutney* (see p. 68).

Makhane Ki Kheer

Sweet thickened milk with lotus seeds

Preparation time: 30 min.
Cooking time: 2 hr.
Serves: 4-6

Ingredients:

Lotus seeds (*makhane*)	1 cup / 200 gm
Water	1¼ cups / 250 ml
Milk	10 cups / 2 lt
Sugar	1 cup / 200 gm

Method:

1. Boil the lotus seeds in the water. Leave to simmer for half an hour.
2. Boil the milk in a wok (*kadhai*). Simmer for half an hour or till it becomes thick.
3. Add the lotus seeds and cook for about 5 minutes.
4. Add the sugar and stir till it dissolves completely. Remove from the fire; pour into a serving dish and chill.

Note: Can also be served hot.

Desserts

Lapsi
Sweet porridge with broken wheat

Preparation time: 15 min.
Cooking time: 30 min.
Serves: 4-6

Ingredients:

Broken wheat (*dalia*)	1 cup / 200 gm
Clarified butter (*ghee*)	½ cup / 100 gm
Aniseeds (*saunf*)	1 tsp / 5 gm
Almonds (*badam*), blanched,	
halved	8-10
Dry coconut (*copra*), slivers	1 tbsp / 15 gm
Water	3 cups / 600 ml
Sugar	½ cup / 100 gm
Green cardamoms	
(*choti elaichi*), crushed	4

Method:

1. Heat the clarified butter in a wok (*kadhai*). Add the aniseed and let them crackle.
2. Add the broken wheat and stir-fry till it is well browned.
3. Add the almonds, coconut and water; bring to a boil.
4. Lower the flame and cook till the broken wheat becomes tender.
5. Add the sugar and stir till it dissolves completely.
6. Remove from the flame, garnish with a few slivers of almonds and cardamoms.

Kesar Kulfi

Rich creamy ice-cream

Ingredients:

Milk	10 cups / 2 lt
Sugar	1⅛ cups / 225 gm
Rose water (*gulabjal*)	5 drops
Pistachios (*pista*), blanched, slivered	2 tbsp / 30 gm
Saffron (*kesar*)	a pinch
Green cardamoms (*choti elaichi*), powdered	½ tsp / 3 gm

Method:

1. Boil the milk in a wok (*kadhai*); lower the flame and stir constantly for 15 minutes. Thereafter, stir after every 5 minutes, until the milk is reduced to less than half its original quantity and acquires a granular texture.

2. Remove from the fire; add the sugar, rose water, pistachios, saffron soaked in 1 tbsp of milk and the green cardamoms. Stir till the sugar dissolves and then cool. Pour this mixture into *kulfi*/cone-shaped moulds and cover. Freeze for atleast 8-10 hours, to allow it to set well.

3. To unmould, open the lid, run a knife along the insides of the moulds and invert onto a serving dish. Alternately, dip the moulds (lid closed) into a pan of water, hold for a few seconds and then invert onto the serving dish.

4. Cut into pieces and serve immediately, sprinkled with rose syrup.

Desserts

Suggested Menus

Non-vegetarian

Safed Maas (*Exotic lamb curry*)	10
Degchi Soola Murgh (*Smoked chicken*)	22

or

Vegetarian

Daal-Bati-Choorma	26
(*Pulses-bread-dessert delight*)	
Papad Ki Sabzi (*Sun-dried wafers in curry*)	46

Accompaniments

Mangodi Pulao	52
(*Fried rice with green gram dumpling*)	
Pyaz Ka Raita	72
(*Yoghurt flavoured with fried onions*)	

Dessert

Kesar Kulfi (*Rich creamy ice-cream*)	90

Non-vegetarian

Laal Maas (*Red, hot lamb curry*)	16
Sabut Murgh (*Dry whole chicken*)	20

or

Vegetarian

Gatte Ka Saag	45
(*Steamed gram flour dumplings in spicy gravy*)	
Makki Ki Sabzi (*Spicy corn*)	38

Accompaniments

Bajre Ki Roti (*Millet flour unleavened bread*)	56
Kachoomber/Choori (*Fresh salad*)	74

Dessert

Makhane Ki Kheer	86
(*Sweet thickened milk with lotus seeds*)	

Glossary of Cooking Terms

Marinade — A seasoned mixture of oil, vinegar, lemon juice, etc, in which meat, poultry, fish is left for sometime to soften its fibres and add flavours to it.

Roast — Cook in an oven or in open heat.

Sauté — Fry quickly over strong heat in fat or oil.

Simmer — Keep boiling gently on low heat.

Stir-fry — Fry rapidly while stirring and tossing.

Smoke — The process of imparting a smoked flavour to the preparation. Heat a piece of coal over the flame till it becomes red hot. Overlap 2-3 onion peels to form a small cup. Place it in the dish, in the middle of the preparation to be smoked. Place the coal in the onion-peel cup. Smoke with either of the following:

1. Smoking with garlic paste: Put ½ tsp of garlic (*lasan*) paste on the coal. Pour 1 tsp of clarified butter (*ghee*) on it. Immediately cover with a lid and smoke for 5-7 minutes.

2. Smoking with cloves: Put 3 cloves on the coal. Immediately cover with a lid, smoke for 5-7 minutes.

3. Smoking with clarified butter: Put 1 tsp of clarified butter on the coal. Immediately cover with a lid and smoke for 5-7 minutes. For best results, this process must be done quickly, so it helps to have everything handy.

Index

ISBN: 81-7436-125-1

© **Roli Books Pvt. Ltd. 2000**
Lustre Press Pvt. Ltd.
M-75, Greater Kailash-II Market,
New Delhi-110 048, INDIA
Phones: (011) 6442271, 6462782, 6460886
Fax: (011) 6467185, E-mail: roli@vsnl.com
Website: rolibooks.com

Photographs: Dheeraj Paul

Printed and bound in Singapore